First published in Australia by HiveMind Press 2023.

Copyright © HiveMind Press, 2023.

Dave Innes has asserted his moral right under the Copyright Act 1968, [2006], and Patents Act 1990, to be identified as the author of this work.

All rights reserved. No reproduction, copy or transmission of this publication may be made without written permission. No paragraph of this publication may be reproduced, copied or transmitted save with written permission or in accordance with the provsisions of the Copyright Act 1968, [2006]. Any person who does any unauthorised act in relation to this publication may be liable to criminal prosecution and civil claims for damages.

ISBN: 978-1-923053-03-8

Typeset/Cover Design by - HiveMind Press.

REFLECTIONS OF A WANDERER

Poems of the Road Less Traveled

Dave Innes

Contents

Been Fishing	1
A Smile	2
Confusion	3
Another Sleepless Night	5
But If	6
Coony Saloony *	7
Drivel	8
For a Start	9
Day One *	10
For Stella	12
Gadge *	13
Oh! For a good nights sleep	15
'Mikayla'	16
An Armful of Dags	17
Heritage	18
Hitch	19
Join The Army	20
As I see it now	21
Lady *	22
Loui et Louise *	23
Mudge	25
Fading Reflection	26
Midnight Blues	27
A Minute	28
'My Father'	29
My Ma	30
My Song	31
Nabiru 2	33
Downtown Darkan	35
Swanee Calapso	37

Contents

The Preservation of Man	39
Suzy	40
Nambi	41
Our Garden	42
Nabiru	43
Thongs	45
Pay Day	46
This Book	47
Wishing *	48
"Sachet La foil'	49
Redheughs	50
Stagnating *	52
Street Kid.	53
Strolling	54
Take Your City	55
The Australind	56
Straight Sunday	57
The Character Jim	58
The Frog	59
Why	60
Time for Bed	61
Sunburn	62
Yes Sir and Three Bags Full	63
Zen	64
Pay Day 2	65
The Little Lebanese Leprechaun	66
Wha's Like Us	67
The Ravenshoe Line	68
Isn't Life a Bitch	69
Why Wait	70
The Last Six Weeks *	71

"Been Fishing"

My next port of call was Geraldton
I came up for the scallop season
I don't know why, too late, I'm here
Just a momentary lapse of reason.
Came up here, all psyched up
Ready to make quick buck
It's worked before, at least until now
But it's over, nobody gives a fuck.
Five years ago, you could make a quid
Four years ago, was a bit worse
Three and two years ago we were scratching around
And last year was a fisherman's curse.
So, I don't know why I bothered this year
I had a hunch there was nothing out there
I won't be back for any more seasons
Cos it seems that no one does care,
that they're fishing it out, it's drying up,
Just trawl and trawl again, it would appear.
All out for the dollar, right here, right now
They don't seem to care about next year.
So, I'll stick to the sheds, where works guaranteed
And the lifestyle lives up to its name,
I like the life and I'm getting too old,
Time to give up the fishing game,
It's a phase of life, one that I have enjoyed
One of the best of my life, I would say
So, I'll toddle off and go back to me sheds
And I'll see you down the pub one day.

A Smile
by Pat Miller

I had a smile
I gave that smile away
The milkman and the postman
Seemed glad of it each day

I took it out while shopping
I had it in the street
I gave it without thinking
To all I chanced to meet

I gave the little ones my smile
And though I'd much to do
I gave it to my neighbours
The old folks had it too

I always gave my smile away
As thoughtless as could be
Yet every time how wonderfully
My smile returned to me

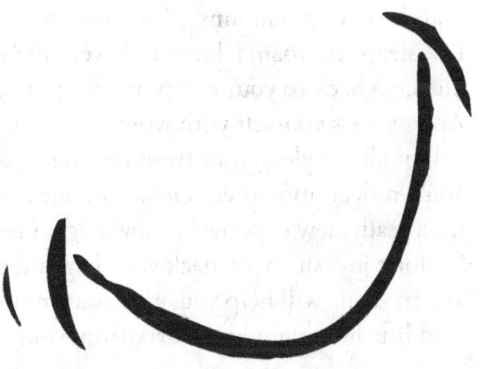

Confusion

Poetry for me is a means of self expression,
A release for my good and bad frustrations,
But at times my mind stops working and becomes stagnant
So I retreat into my shell, like a crustacean.
I can write about the good times, the fun things in life
Or my hatred for the cities that I've seen,
I can write without thinking, let my pen do all the work
And tell of scenery or places that I've been.
My personal feelings are not written in my verse,
Except for the beautiful lady by my side,
Although a little part of me goes in with every word
I can still be me; I do not have to hide.
If you could read between the comma's and see it as I do,
I don't suppose you can cos' you're not me,
You'd see about the places dreamed of far away,
Of places that one day you may see.
So, forget about the city, your job and whatnot mate,
Go out and see what it is really like,
Have a look around you, absorb the countryside,
Pack up your swag and, literally, take a hike.
Wander over mountains; pick mushies in the dale,
Eat, sleep and roam all day and every night,
Then, go back to your camping spot put your pen to work
And express yourself with words that you will write.
Tell of all the glory your fresh new body feels,
You'll reflect upon these memories one day,
It's a really new experience, never again to be found
So don't just sit there, pack your bag and get away.
The fresh air will help you; give your mind an overhaul
And lift the weight and worry from your aching back,

You'll feel like a new person, the old one left behind,
You'll feel so good you won't want to come back.
I might see you out there, one bright and sunny day,
We could cross paths upon the mountain slope,
It could be in the mushie field or at the local inn,
Somewhere out there where both of us can cope.
So I hope that you keep smiling and are happy all the time
In that place where dreams and realities materialise,
Do the things you want to, let your mind run free,
When I see you there one day then I will realise.
That you have found your utopia, the place you really need,
To relax and let your emotions shine on through,
Where nothing really matters and time's not of the essence
Where I am me and you are really you.

Another Sleepless Night

Analytic images crashing through the gums,
Lying here in awe until the next one comes.
No moon tonight, no ultraviolet illusion,
Close your eyes, see its face, it's an hallucination.
The falseness of night, the dark of the eve
It's amazing what games the mid plays,
How the imagination can perceive.
The breeze comes through
To change the perfect picture,
Of serenity, of peace the perfect scenario,
The wind alters the tincture.
Then daylight comes, the images fade
And sanity starts to regather,
When it's all gone and day is done,
Tonight, I'll sleep, I'd rather.

But If

Well, drugs and alcohol are not supposed to mix
Whether fanging for a drink or hanging for a fix.
But one leads to another, they go hand in hand,
Be it drinking or otherwise, they're both in demand.
If you start on the booze it slows you up a bit,
If you go for the needle you don't want no shit.
When you just want a smoke, it's just not enough
You'll eventually end up on some other stuff.
A snort or a taste just to get off your face
Booze and pot just don't keep up the pace.
Snort it, blast it, drop it or squirt,
You'll always end up with your face in the dirt.
It's good while it lasts but you must come down
If you fall off the boardwalk, be ready to drown.
Sink or swim as the old saying goes
Whether it goes in your arm or stuffed up your nose.
Your lungs get cloggy, your liver gives out
And after a while it loses it's clout.
You need more and more, your tolerance builds up
Whether drinking, smoking or shooting it up.
So leave it alone, I'm sure you'll agree
If you don't know what you're doing, stay drug free.
If you've been there, done that, got bored and moved on
Be happy to stick to some booze and your bong.
'cos new highs are pretty hard to come by
and if you haven't been there, don't try to fly.
Sit back, relax and take day by day
Don't let your addiction carry you away.
If you can't go flying, leave your wings at home,
Don't try it, don't do it, just leave it alone.

Coony Saloony *

We travelled up to Geraldton
In the good old coon saloon
And when we become civilised
That will be too soon

To sleep at the beach
With the wind blowing strong
The seaweed stinks
It's a hell of a pong

The journey up here
Was a hell of a trip
We got bogged, had a blowout
And the driver did flip.

We lived like coons
On the side of the road
The roof rack's an arse
We nearly lost our load.

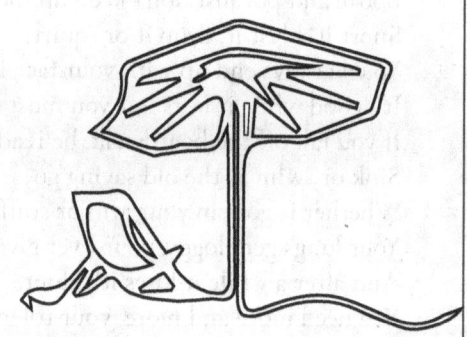

But we'll fish and be happy
We're here for the duration
We might live like blacks
But we've had education

So leave us alone
And we'll let you be
We're white aboriginals stay with us and see.

But we're happy little vegemites
Living the way we do
It's our way of life
We've done it, have you.

Drivel

Well, here we are on a cool Sunday night,
Watching two men on the screen have a fight,
It's the Bunbury drive-in with Superman Three,
We can't hear a thing but there's plenty to see.

The mozzies are bad, the winds blowing fresh
Not the best of conditions, I'm just not impressed
The tent is all saggy, it might fall down
My back's nearly broken from the hard, lumpy ground.

No gas in the bottle, no food to prepare
If we had meat to eat it would be done quite rare.
But things are not the worst that they've ever been
out here in the open; watching the screen.

But that's another story, yet to be told,
It's beddy bye time, it's getting too cold.
Tomorrows a new day, yet to be seen
I hope it's better than what's been on the screen.

No violence, no hailstorm, no wounded or maimed,
This poem's pathetic, not worth being named.

For a Start

Life on the dole is not what it seems
You'll never fulfill just one of your dreams.
No money to spend, so little to do,
I've done this before, why, haven't you?.
So much per week, not enough to survive,
The queue at the counter at quarter to five.
The rent's overdue, no food for the kids,
You feel so hopeless, you'd pawn life for quids.
Report and do this just like a machine,
They know nothing of a place never been.
No sense of adventure, no will to explore
This place they've heard so much of before.
We struggle for money and food to get by,
When the hardship goes in, an occasional lie.
But for two days a week we just have to fast
Waiting for the next seven or eight to go past.
In numbers you're okay, alone you are sunk
There ain't enough money to even get drunk.
Enough for the bills and bingo each week
By the year 2000 there'll be tax on a leak.
No need to worry, no need to sweat,
No grey hairs and no need to fret.
So apply for the dole, it's good fun, you'll see
And play instant survival, just like me.

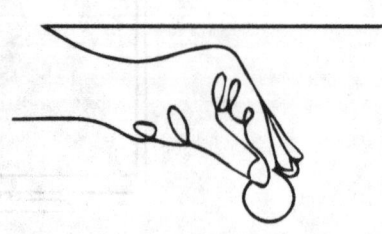

Day One *

We have a little flat,
not big, but it's ours
About one hundred feet above the ground
Our little love nest towers

When you look out the window
You get quite a view
This area, to my lady
Is relatively new

I don't know it that well
But I'm sure that we'll find out
If we go for a walk
And have a bit of a scout

To check where the pub is
The shops and the train
We've got a roof above us now
To keep out the driving rain

No more river banks
No more sleazy pubs
No more noisy traffic
No more sharing tubs

For this is for us two
With no-one to share
If I was one of them
I don't think I'd dare

This is our sanity
Our own little haven
A place for which too long
We've always been cravin'

We'll leave you alone
If you let us be
And the rest of the story,
Babe, I think you can see

<u>Mosman Park April 84</u>

For Stella

If I could catch a rainbow
I would do it just for you
And share with you its beauty
On the days your feeling blue

If I could build a mountain
You could call your very own
A place to find serenity
A place to be alone

If I could take your troubles
And toss them in the sea
But all these things I'm finding
Are impossible to me

I cannot build a mountain
Or catch a rainbow fair
But let me do what I do best
And be a friend that's always there

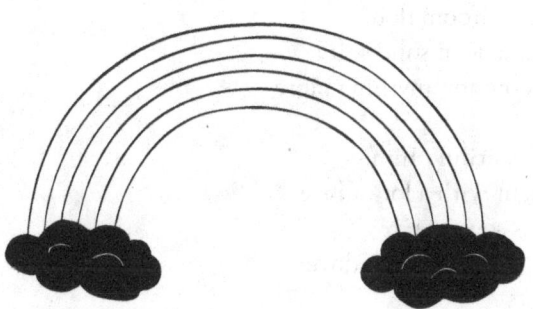

Gadge *

Whilst out shopping last week
With my lovely wife beside me
As we walked past the pet shop
a little pup we did see

Lyn fell in love straight away
It didn't take me too long to follow
That little dog fell in love, too
And on his face, it did show

Lyn asked me if I wanted him
As a birthday present from her
That dog is a lovechild
I couldn't refuse the offer

Well, we christened the little pup Gadge
He's like an albino rat
He's really made himself at home
As on the bed he shat

He shits from arsehole to breakfast time
All over the bedroom floor
He must be made of solid shit
There's no room for anything more

But he is a beautiful canine
He was bought with a lot of love
A love that is so very rare
It's soft, like the wings of a dove.

He's learning fast what not to do
He's learning to shit outside
And wherever myself and my true love go
He'll be right there, by our side

<u>Mt Hawthorn 84</u>

"Oh! For a good nights sleep"

He was lying on his bed at the end of the day
And he thought he'd go to sleep, or so he did say.
So the light grew dim as the candle burnt out
Then the first possum came; he was just a scout.
Then the second and his mate did venture in the barn,
Whilst in the mans head, off went an alarm.
There was a flurry for the matches to get the candle lit
While he grappled in the dark, looking for his stick.
The first was on the cupboard, staring at the glow
As the man rounded the corner, how did he know?
And the possum silently vanished; he had places to go.
By then, the second possum knew what was being done
So he headed for the window with a stick hard at his bum.
The third possum's on the mans bed,
Just daring to hazard a copping,
And to be caught on the wall on the way to the door,
By geez, he took a whopping.
And so the place was quiet again as the man began to yawn
'Twas time to go back to bed, at least until the dawn.
It seemed an hour ago since he last lay in his cot
As he nestled down amongst his rugs, trying to get hot.
"I showed them beasts a thing or two," his conscience proudly beams
And so another day is done goodnight Michael, sweet dreams.

'Mikayla'

Well done, my good lady, she's finally here,
You've waited so long for this girl to appear.
Congrat's are in order, I'm sure you'll agree
That this is the moment you've waited to see.
The birth of your baby is really worthwhile,
It's good, It's great just to see your beautiful smile.
This lady has waited so long for this day,
What you mean to her, I hope and I pray.
For you are her treasure, her one and her own,
The joy you've brought Kathy will never be known.
May the good Lord watch over you each step of the way,
'cos He knows the happiness you have brought on this day.
Your mother, my friend, my eternal soul mate,
Is wonderful, loving and it is on this date
That she will remember the love that you bring,
For the person you are is no little thing.
So I give you my blessings, my dear little friend,
And I hope that our friendship never does end.
And on life's adventure, you're off to explore,
With your Mum on your side, you'll need never more.
Be careful, be wise and keep your eyes open
And may you get everything you want, at least I'm hopin'.

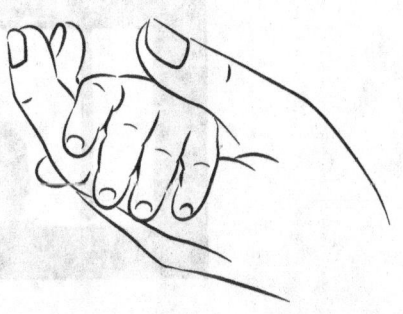

An Armful of Dags

Just to sit alone in the shearing shed,
It's the weekend, with no-one else there,
No sheep in the pens, no wool on the board,
Look around you, it's all pretty bare.
Yet to think how many sheep go through here,
They come in, they go round, they go out,
A shitload of wool, A bucketful of sweat
And an armful of dags to sort out.
But now it's all quiet, the machinery's still,
Not a sound to be heard through the place,
Yet come Monday morn. At 7:30 sharp,
It'll be on, to see who sets the pace.
So, with your armful of dags and a smile on your dial,
You battle through just one more run,
Pick it up, throw it, skirt it and move
After all, you're not here for fun.
Yet the nights and the weekends, they're something else,
There's no rules banned in this game,
Get a lungful of smoke, get pissed, go to bed,
'cos tomorrow's gonna be just the same.

Heritage

In days gone by, before Cook and his mates,
The land was at peace with dingoes and primates.
I'll bet they were surprised when the aboriginal saw
All those funny white men, down on the shore.
Were they good, were they bad, where were they from?
What had they to fear from the exploring pom?
He tried to trade goods and show them some charm
But the blacks wouldn't wear it, they raised the alarm.
The woomeras flew, the start of a fight,
One that went on for many a night.
The blood flowed freely, Cook paid the cost,
The blacks knew this fight was not to be lost.
Cook had no right to this land for his own,
He was in the wrong country, wrong place, wrong zone.
Still more people came and convicts as well,
To the shores of Australia, to settle and dwell.
The aboriginal kept fighting for what it appears
Was theirs by right, to be fought for with spears.
All men alike should live side by side
They tried this, it didn't work, somebody'd lied.
And the blacks were pushed onto hot open plains
So whitey could prosper and increase his gains.
Two hundred years later, the aboriginals still fight
For what they know to be theirs by right.
And they will keep fighting for what is their own,
How it will end will never be known.
If I was a black man I would have fought too,
They're Australia's heritage, I think so, don't you.

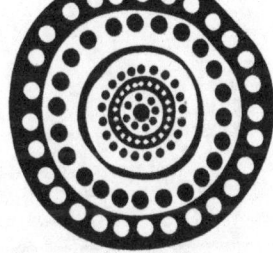

Hitch

If you don't know where you're going
Don't expect anyone else to say
Why not go up to such and such
They'll probably point you the wrong way.
You should go out and discover
The different ways to travel,
You can drive, fly, sail or train it
But if you hitch, the roads will unravel.
No one way tickets, no returns will be needed,
You just follow the road 'til the end,
Why sit back and think of it?
You've got legs, no need to pretend.
To follow a never ending highway,
To follow the eternal white line,
Just follow the coast, it goes on forever,
See your country, I've been and seen mine.
So, make sure you're heading the right way
Just your backpack and thumb you will need
To meet all kinds of beings
You'll find out about poverty and greed.
It'll make you grow up and open your eyes,
Let you see things you've never before
You'll have both good and bad times, mostly good,
So try it, you'll love it I'm sure.

Join The Army

"Join the army" they said,
learn a trade, move ahead,
it's an exciting life as you will surely see,
get promoted, see the world,
shoot a commie, get a girl,
and in the jungle is where you'll surely be.
To fight another man's battle,
One you know nothing about,
To be stalked by the unknown and the unseen,
To lie there in the darkness
And wonder who'll be next,
You'll find out when you hear a deathly scream.
So go and join the army
See the world and shoot a man,
Just see how much you take before you crack,
Go fight for your country
And hold that flag up high
And I'll see you all when you come marching back.

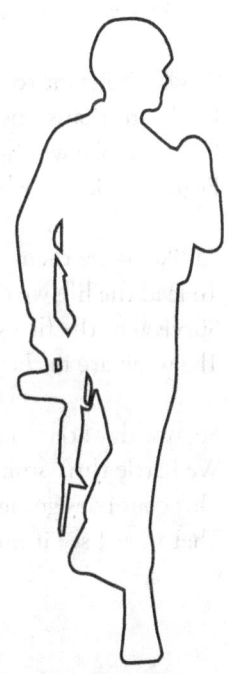

As I see it now

As I see it now,
This country's sure in strife,
No work and no money,
Not much of a life.

All the time you're struggling
To live one day at a time
No money, no job existence
Is almost a bloody crime.

Seventy-four a week
For food and rent and bills,
No money to do what you want to,
Survival, without the frills.

"It wasn't meant to be easy",
I've heard that somewhere before
From a bloke who was ripping off money
From the rich, the battlers and poor.

I'd like to see them do it
To lead the life we do
Survival of the fittest
The weak are in the pooh.

So, one day at a time
We battle thru, somehow,
This countries going to pieces
That is, as I see it now.

Lady *

Monday night, the sun going down
A beautiful lady beside,
We've had a swim and woken up now,
Back to the place we reside.

To feel her charms and hold her close
To hear of the beauties beyond
This lady of mine, the one I adore,
Who is gentle, loving and kind.

Who looks after me and watches me close
Who thinks of the things I have seen
To follow me to a place of despair,
a place that she's never been.

I love this lady, she's one of a kind
Never to be found once again
And if I lost her now for evermore
I think I would think twice again.

For she is a lass and one of a kind
I've never found one such before
And if I had my way for eternity
I'm as happy as never before.

If we should part for reasons unknown
And never again to be seen
She always will be a part of my
never ending, elusive dream.

Coronation Beach WA Feb 84

Loui et Louise *

He sits on the top floor
In the corner he huddles
She comes up occasionally
Just for kisses and cuddles

Then those kisses and cuddles
Became something more
For there's five little babies
Down on the ground floor

Now, Loui is the black one
With the piercing, black, wee eyes
Who scampers down the ladder
When he hears the young one's cries

He's always in the corner
Where he sleeps away the day
He pisses in the other one
Which don't half stink, I'll say

Louise is the fawn runaround
The one with the waltzing hop
When she's let out to exercise
You'll see she rarely does stop

One minute she destroys the nest she's built
The next she'll be trying to rebuild
But she looks after her kids, the babies
Whose eyes are closed and fat bellies filled

So, we'll let them be, our two little mates
They've got plenty of food to suffice
To run around and live as they do
Our pets, our two little mice

Mosman Park WA May 84

Mudge

There's a bloke I know from NSW
Who's been over here for a while
His humour is infectious
And he's usually wearing a smile

No matter what the odds are
He'll always give it a try
From highest of high to lowest of low
Mudge always seems to get by

We've had to walk a mile or two
To find an outback dunny
And once, when we were oh so close
He did not think that was funny

I could go on and spin a yarn
About this bloke, my mate, blah, blah
And I hope we never hear the echo
Of Rah, Rah, fucking Rah

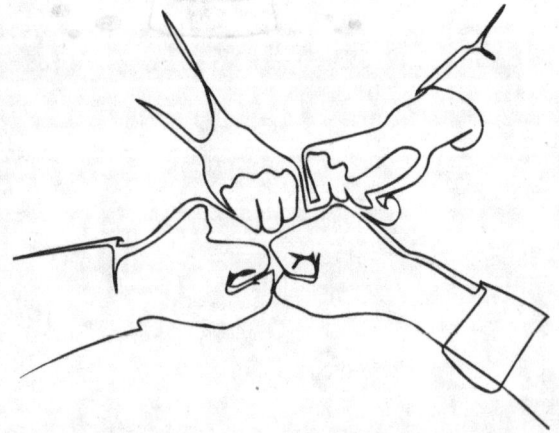

Fading Reflection

Well, I've got nothing to show for the last twenty years
I've been full on as an alcoholic
I've been here, been there, done this, done that
it all seems to be quite diabolic.
To have lived this long, to have seen so much
to have enjoyed life all the way,
ain't got many teeth but I still smile a lot,
and I really don't care what they say.
This is my life, I'll do as I please
don't have to answer to no-one at all,
the last twenty years, just been cruisin' around,
doing my own thing and having a ball.
I don't own a house, haven't got two- point five kids
no mortgage, no hire purchase, no trouble
and if I had my time all over again
I'd have twice as much fun, doing it double.
But time goes on, getting older, occasionally think
of all the things I could've had if I hadn't taken to drink
yet it's too late for that, reflections fade out,
but I have had a bloody good time, without a doubt.

Midnight Blues

While I wait at night for sleep to occur
The wind and the trees outside do stir,
Nothing to see but the dog at the window,
Is he myth or reality, what does he know?
As he lies in the box with a grin on his face
Has he been here before, here, to this place?
With a scratch and a fleabite, a quick shuffle round
He goes off to sleep on the soft sandy ground.
The image in the window is something to see,
It looks pretty damn much like me,
The same moustache, the same curly hair,
The same tattoos and the same blank stare.
But what does he know this image in the glass?
Perhaps of the future, perhaps of the past,
Nobody knows the answer to this,
If they do they must be in pure, peaceful bliss.
But the dead tell no lies and have nothing to hide,
Yet us live ones do, we all have lied,
For good or for bad, it don't really matter
'Cos the poor stay poor and the rich get fatter.
Not one of us is perfect if the truth be told
If you claim you are, you must be bold.
But then again, there are those whose cries
Can be heard, telling those little white lies.
Been there, done that, got bored and moved on
But to where, no one knows, it goes on and on.
It makes you wonder what you should do,
So steer clear of the cemetery, I've been there, have you?

A Minute

Life is just a minute,
Only sixty seconds in it,
Forced upon you, can't refuse it,
Didn't seek it, didn't choose it
But it's up to you to use it.
You must suffer if you lose it,
Give an account if you abuse it.
Just a tiny little minute but eternity is in it.

'My Father'

I know this man, well I've known him all my life,
Who's lived all his life for his kids and his wife.
Four kids and a good wife, what more could you ask,
Even though a few of us are a pain in the arse.
His patience is long, His smile's always on,
He's never got a bad word for no~one,
He's worked all His life for His kith and kin,
And he's given laughter, good times and fun.
Most days He goes for a bit of a trot,
Sometimes around the city, sometimes around the block.
He's always been fit, He works and He jogs,
And now He's off to go running with frogs.
But He'll slow down when the time is right,
He won't have to go running each morning and night.
His body will tell Him enough is enough,
And He'll have to give up all this physical stuff.
'tis time to sit back and enjoy life's pleasure,
you've worked hard and long, 'tis time for your leisure.
And it is on this day that you're sixty~five'
I give thanks to God that you were my eyes.
May your long life have good years, none of them bad,
You are the Man that I proudly call DAD.

My Ma

What can I say about my dear sweet Ma
That hasn't been said before?
Well, there are a few things, I reckon
'cos I'm her son, I know a bit more

The lady that I speak of
The lady I adore
Has not only been a mother to me
She has always been much, much more

Ma's always been my friend
My adviser, whenever the need
Ma's always been there when I need her
With a cuppa, a cuddle or a feed

She sometimes gets cross, not very oft
With "I'll put you over my knee"
"you'll never be too big, you know"
"just keep going and you'll soon see"

And now I'm getting on in life
With a different point of view
I think to myself "how did you cope, Ma?"
Then I remember that you are you

The lady that I respect, the one that I love
Is as strong as the bond of no other
Happy birthday, dear Ma, many more to come
For you are the lady I proudly call "Mother"

<u>All my love, always, Dave</u>

My Song

by Pat Miller

Just a line to say I'm living
That I'm not among the dead
Tho I'm getting more forgetful
And mixed up in my head

I've got used to my arthritis
To my dentures I'm resigned
I can manage with my bifocals
But, God, I miss my mind

Sometimes I can't remember
When I'm standing by the stairs
If I'm going up for something
Or have I just come down from there

And before the fridge so often
My mind is filled with doubt
Now, did I just put some food away?
Or did I come to take it out

Sometimes when it is night time
With my nightcap on my head
I don't know if I'm retiring
Or just getting out of bed

So, remember I do love you
And I wish that you were here
But now it's time to mail this
And say goodbye, my dear

At last I stand before the mailbox
My face I'm sure is red
Instead of mailing this to you
I've opened it instead

Nabiru 2

"Dug this fucking big 'ole"
"musta been six foot round"
"put in five deep fried Mars Bars"
"and 'eaded for higher ground"

"I went for a walk"
"Emu came to"
"Had me Plat and me shovel"
"and along came Roo"

'There was this big old tree"
"thought I'd look behind 'er"
"twas then I came face to face"
"with a deadly Wolf Spider"

Oh fuck, thinks Dave,
What to do?
I can't plait a puss
And use me shovel, too!

Then he looked into its face
All hair and teeth and gristle
'twas then he remembered his training
Go for the fuckin' whistle

Well, he puffed and he blew
'Til the whistle was hot
The Emu went deaf
Spider, dead on the spot

The Burmese re-packed, time to clock up some miles
Had to go, he had a few things to do
And I'll always remember that bushman called "Pom"
I'll always know him as "me mate" "Nabiru"

<u>Namesake</u>

Downtown Darkan

Well, I worked in a team down in Darkan
and, mate, let me tell you this
I met a good crew of guys, shearers and such
and by jingo, could they drink some piss.
There was cutouts here and cutouts there
and cutouts every bloody where
when a bloke would try to get to bed
shit no, there's a cutout first day of the shed.
On stand number one there's the Beaver,
by jeez, could he eat his tucker,
yet give him a rousie with the old slide broom
and he'd spend eight hours a day trying to fuck her.
On stand number two was the Bushie
the responsible one amongst us,
he'd only have four cans on the way home
but that's only because he was driving the bus.
Then on number three was the Gavin,
he'd do sixty a run in full flight,
but it's got me fucked how he works all day
with the amount of piss he drinks every night.
Last but not least we have TJ
who's evenings were kept quite obscure
but when he came in for a night on the piss
there'd be hangovers all round, for sure.
Now, let's not forget the young Guesser
what job he had is still quite a riddle,
but he threw the wool around and counted them out
and somehow got the name Mr Squiggle.
And the grey haired old man in the corner
is really a pretty good sport,

he'll start off on the O.J., turn on to the beer,
guaranteed to end up on port.
The man in the white hats a real gentleman
he'll cough and he'll burp and he'll fart,
but I know for a fact that he's true blue
and he's got a bloody big heart.
Yet the man who is partly to blame
for this staggered, drunken procession,
who'd put six free jugs of beer on the bar
and lock us in after the session.
The man who sold us such drinks
to allow us to   get into this state,
should be given great honour and a pat on the back
good on ya, Graham, and thanks old mate.
Then there's Dave, the pissy old gift wrapper
who's had fun all the time he was here,
I know I've had a ball and drank my share of piss
so I'll see ya all, same time, next year.

Swanee Calapso

Down by the Swanee river
Where the seagulls feed and play
We sit and drink our goonie
That's all we do all day.

We sit in the lounge
And talk and drink
When we're out of calapso
It's hard to think

Two dollars Fifty for half a G
We do that thrice a day
There's only one big problem
We just can't give it away.

It's a way of life
Something to do
If we didn't drink
We'd be just like you.

Six litres a day
 of clarrie and rose
I don't know where we would be,
up shit creek, I s'pose

If we didn't have the habit
We didn't have to drink
I couldn't handle being straight
I'd go insane, I think.

So I will keep on grogging
Until my dying day

Which might be in the near future
If I carry on this way.

So let's all drink and be happy
We only have one life
And if you, old son, can't be jovial
Then, brother, you're in strife.

Coronation Beaach WA Feb 84

The Preservation of Man

by Anon***

The horse and mule live for thirty years
And know nothing of wine and beers
The goat and sheep at twenty dies
With never a taste of Scotch or Rye

The cow drinks water by the ton
And at eighteen is almost done
The dog, at sixteen cashes in
Without the aid of Rum or Gin

The cat in milk and water soaks
And then in twelve short years it croaks
The modest, sober, bone dry hen
Lays eggs for nogs then dies at ten

All animals are strictly dry
They live sinless and swiftly die
But sinful, ginful, rum soaked men
Survive for three score years and ten

And some of us, the mighty few
Stay pickled 'til we're ninety-two

Suzy

There's a pub in downtown Geraldton
Down the road, in the main street,
Where friends gather and drink and such
And the barmaid can't be beat.
A little lass, petite, I'd say,
She even puts it in for me
With a smile that's very contagious
She's the best, is little Suzy.
Suzy will stop and chat and say "good-day"
And ask how your weekend went
Then you'll reply, "Well, I got pissed"
"And hell, did I get bent."
So off she twats to serve someone else
And then she'll be back again
To give you shit and make you smile,
She's not just a barmaid; she's a friend.
So you take care, little lady,
And I'll see you down the track,
Be good, stay happy and stay beautiful,
And I'll catch you down the track.

Nambi

The generator cranks up, the sun is on the way
Out here in desert country, the start of a new day
The shed is full of sheep, ready to be shorn
The cook is in the kitchen, brewing up some chorn

The early morning coughs and farts, as regular as birds
The line up for the dunny, to expel unwanted turds
The twin tub working overtime to get rid of grease and dust
Jack wants to get off his chain, he looks fit to bust

Brekkie over, boots on, bandana round the head
Time to go for a walk, but only as far as the shed
Day thirteen at Nambi will be like the twelve just passed
Shear more sheep, light the donkey, isn't life a blast

One more day, maybe three and we'll be on the track
Back to civilisation and family, but next year we'll be back
To put up with the prickles, the dust and dreaded mozz
You ask why we do this, the answers just because

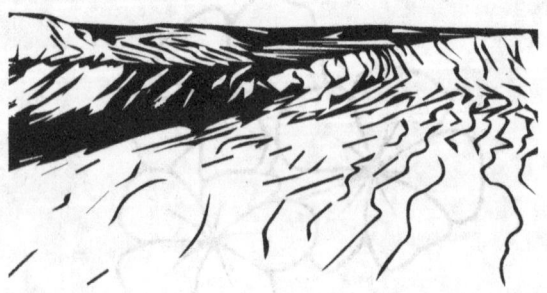

Our Garden

by Anon

The heart is a garden where thought flowers grow
The thoughts that we think
Are the seeds that we sow.
Every kind loving thought
Bears a kind loving deed
While the thought that is selfish
Is just like a weed.
We must watch what we think
Each minute, all day,
And pull out the weed thoughts
And throw them away.
And plant loving seed thoughts
So thick in a row,
That there won't be room
For weed thoughts to grow.

Nabiru

The table was jumping
The ground it did quiver
Things started moving
The chill, a quick shiver

The wind died off
The air was still
If you looked to the south
'Twas coming over the hill

Dust storms and lightning
God knows where from
Well fuck, no, it can't be
It's the bushman called "Pom"

He was riding side-saddle
On his trusty Burmese
Bouncing along
With the greatest of ease

When the dust settled down
And y'd get a lungful of air
He'd pull off his chappers
And pull up a chair

Beer in hand "orright Davo?"
"Not bad, Nabiru, how'd yours go?"
"Orright, not bad, you know how it is"
"The snakes are bad, the Bears, piece of piss"

"A hoopsnake got wind of me"
"As I was coming down the hill'

"But me Platypus was onto it"
"Give me the signal with his bill"

Good thing I greased me shovel
Thought the Pommie from the bush
Time to pull up, get off
And put me Platypus to use

Thongs

Down here in the land of Koalas and roos,
Half of the people never wear shoes,
For thongs are the go, the "in" thing to wear,
They're comfortable, cheap, with no heels to repair.
There's no need for socks, no laces to tie,
When they're dirty you wash 'em, two minutes to dry.
No toe jams or smells for one to offend
And into the shape of your feet they do bend.
So get some today, they're worth it, you'll see,
Get rid of your shoes, let your feet run free.
No dirt under your nails, no germs to breed
So slap 'em on, wear 'em round,
 You'll like 'em, agreed?

Pay Day

It's getting light, the day has come
Time to move, to be there by eight
Out into the cold, to wait at the bus stop
It's time for the fortnightly wait

It's Tuesday again, dole form day
The chromosome brown 19b
Put the brain into overdrive
What yarn can we spin, let me see

The rents run aground, the cupboards are bare
The kids got no shoes on their feet
The toilet's blocked and the fridge don't work
Just think of a good one, you're sweet

Fill out the form, and hand it in
Take a seat and they'll check ya out
So you sit and wonder, will they or not
'course they will but there's always a doubt

You didn't get a counter cheque last time
So everything should work out fine
But the two before that were paid on the spot
Maybe I'm wasting my time

Your name is called, the hopes arise
You look a sour cow in the face
A yes or a no will suffice, if you please
So I can get out of this place

She hums and haws, then picks her nose
She looks at your file and says
"you realise that if we give you it now
It'll have to last you sixteen days"

This Book

This book is written with thoughts that I feel
Very few people understand
I'd rather write them down as they come to mind
Don't like to use thoughts second hand

This little black books like a diary
Except I don't write every day
My thoughts are written as they come
Anyplace, wherever, any day

This is a lot of emotion
There's also a lot of fun
But for every poem I've ever wrote
I've experienced every one

So you can take your poems of myth
Of pretence, make believe or your dreams
But try to relate the things that you feel
It's really twice as hard as it seems

I won't write of bullshit, of things I don't know
Or experiences yet to be felt
I write what I feel, no need to lie
Of places that I have seen or have dwelt

So you write your prose and let me write mine
At least mine are down to the point
If you don't like it, keep it to yourself
Don't get your nose out of joint

I'll let you be if you let me alone
I try not to hassle no-one
So you do your thing and let me do mine
And you'll find we'll all live as one
Mosman Park WA May 84

Wishing *

I have a wish, a far off dream
In which everything goes our way
Where money is no object
'cos I get a weekly pay

I'm not asking for anything much
Not extravagant or even flash
Just enough to get out of the rut
Of the dole and having no cash

My wish is to get married
And everything's going well
No need to worry about anything else
'cos it can go to hell

But the best of my wish comes later
When the party and good will is over
And I can take Lyn to a place
Where we can romp through fields of green clover

And comfort and leisure are all that we need
In surroundings where we won't smother
Where we don't have to worry about a thing
Except our love and need for each other

As I said before, this is but a dream
It don't hurt to dream now and then
it may come true one day, I hope
don't know if, where or when

But until then, I'll keep on wishing
Of that far distant place that we need
Where everything is as I wish it to be
And comforts our right, not our greed
<u>Broome WA Nov 84</u>

"Sachet La foil"

Up here in the land of Scallies and crays
Where nothing but the weather does spoil
You'll find a man with a smile on his face
And they call him Sachet La Foil.
Where what he does every day is for love and not toil,
He's an Ever-Ready battery, Monsieur Sachet La Foil.
There's not a leaf that can't be matured
There's not a head that can't be turned,
Cause all in all, it's all the same
The whole bloody lot gets burned.
Always on the lookout, is this a possible sale?
"Only six more to go" thinks Sachet La Foil
"And then it's time for an ale"
Down to the pub "Give us a can and make it bloodywell quick,"
He never had much of a way with words
But by jingo, was he slick.
A sachet here, a doily there, 'There's no mates rates today,"
"If you want to smoke this noxious weed,"
"Then full price you will pay."
" I've had my share of all this shit"
"And there's no union in this trade,"
"So cash up front, you know the rules, the bottom lines been laid."
Yet be ye aware, don't go for shit hash oil,
Get the good stuff from Sachet La Foil.
He moves his abode from street to street,
But he haunts the same watering hole,
He sits in the pub and waits for a sale
Near the fire, to keep out of the cold.
But beware; don't cross this masked man,
Don't let his appearance despoil,
Don't mess with this man, beware, be told,
Don't fuck with *Sachet La Foil*

Redheughs

The sun going down, the days at an end
Far away from the maddening crowd,
The wind blowing thru' and singing its song
Just like a translucent cloud.

An occasional car, the caw of a crow,
And from the sheep an infrequent bleat,
The landscape at peace, so quiet and calm
And the clouds spreading out like a sheet.

The fences are here to pen the sheep
But everything else is free
To roam and scrounge for what it can
Round the base of the eucalypt tree.

This is the country, the place to be
To put your mind at rest
And if I had a choice, the city or here,
This is the place I love best.

So, Monday is gone, another day done,
With the sun and the clouds playing games,
The breeze coming thru like a butterfly's fart
All round the distant range

So have a drink and breathe the air,
It's free, at least for now
But don't you worry, they'll think of a way
To tax it for us somehow.

The sound of a laugh, "another beer, please,"
Said Frank to George the Scot

"There's no beer left, so have a Stout,
That's all we've bloody got".

Vasse Wa Jan 84

Stagnating *

I have to give my poems a miss
For just a little while
The one's I'm writing aren't like me
The city's cramped my style

I'm writing about the same old things
I haven't been out much of late
But we're off to Kal in a couple of weeks
I think the break will be great

It'll only be for a couple of days
To see some old friends that I know
We'll get some money and grab the tent
And on the road we will go

I really am feeling quite stagnant
As far as my poetry does wander
We're stuck in the suburbs for a short while
A place where my mind can't meander

All I write of is Lyn and the city
One I love dearly, the other I hate
So before I put anymore in this book
A few weeks, I guess, I'll have to wait

So, I'll hang up my pen
But, hopefully, not for too long
'cos when I've got my pen to paper again
I'll know that's where I belong

<u>Mosman Park April 84</u>

Street Kid.

Three weeks in the city, amid plastic people and cars,
A place like this, this concrete hell, can leave you with terrible scars.
The buses roar past, the ambulance screams,
The paperboys yell out their tune,
If I had a choice, the country or here
I'd be on that road pretty damn soon.
This place that we are, this city of fools
We've seen it all before on tape,
We never thought it really did exist,
Nothing more than pure mental rape.
Some people like it, some people don't
Into the last category we do fall,
People who say they've been to the bush
Are full of shit, they've done stuff all.
But why all the looks, the roundabout swerves,
You'd think we had leprosy it seems,
If they had to live like we've had to do
Just one night, they'd come apart at the seams.
We're tougher than them, we know how to exist
They'd shudder at places we've been
So why put us down, the street kids of Perth,
When they don't know of a place never seen.
We hassle no~one but they hassle us
For reasons unknown to our kind
But whatever the story, the stuck up snobs
I hope it gives them peace of mind.
'cos they're putting us down, the street kids of Perth,
the people who are having bad luck,
they don't really care for the kid on then street,
             in short, they don't give a *fuck*.

Strolling

Whilst strolling through the forest one early Sunday eve,
The sky came over cloudy, 'twas rain I did perceive.
Starlings flocking and feeding in flurries of squealing delight,
The rain sinking into a torrent, leaving no light.
Pine needles being strewn about, the sign of a violent breeze,
To be blown about with the abandon of dandelion seeds.
The trees swaying and whipping each other in the wet,
The rain turning leaf mould into a sodden carpet.
Evil in the shadows, near where innocents play
Taking a thousand forms, most as subtle as snakes.
The rain easing into a patter of individual droplets
Full of the content of satisfied surrender.
Over and around the debris of fallen branches
Decorated with a thousand dew hung cobwebs
Running in ladders and cascades of wet brightness,
In and out of the ivy, up and down the brambles.
The pine smell fresh like new cropped grass,
Sanicle enwrapped in the roots of trees
To open the heart to pride, to fear or to vanity
The grace of whole souled loveliness.
Being drawn forward by a wildflower scent
The shadows receding as the sun shone through
I surrendered my will to the day,
I had nothing better to do.

Take Your City

Lying in our hotel room,
I can hear it but cannot see,
I don't really want to look at it
Nor does my lady with me.

For us it nearly broke up,
That steel and concrete trap
They say the cities beautiful
Well, that's a load of crap.

Trying your all to just exist
Which is almost a bloody crime,
People look at us in the mall
As if we're all sublime.

The cops are pretty nosy
Name, address, date of birth
It's bad news when it's your turn
With others, it is mirth.

We will leave your city
As soon as the time allows
And head for greener pastures
Where no one there will know.

About the troubles we've had
About the things we've seen
And I hope in this place we're heading to
The grass is really green.

So you can take your city
And stick it where it fits
We've had enough of everything
It gives us both the shits.

The Australind

The train pulled out of the city,
Three hours til the end of the line
Due in Bunbury at twelve thirty
The time now half past nine.
Moving out of the suburbs, leaving the city behind
A place that can be callous, ruthless and unkind.
At last, out into the country, where open pastures sprawl
The train is slowing down again, it's almost at a crawl.
A blackboy, burnt and balding just like kojak's head,
The bullrushes still whisper although they're dry and dead.
A gumtree dropping honkey nuts, the homestead fades away,
A dog runs round the paddock as a warm up to the day.
Trees dissected by powerline images, a stile over a disused fence,
Cows waiting at the milking shed, to be fed under false pretence.
Houses appear out the window, the traintrip nearly finished,
The country turns into a suburb, the pastures have diminished.
Concrete, steel and bitumen take over from the green,
To block the open spaces with things you've never seen.

Straight Sunday

So here we are on a Sunday morn
Camping north of town
We're all acting quite troppo
Nothing can bring us down.

The wind is really gusty
The coffee's black as black
And the Leyland Brothers reckon
They went off the beaten track.

"What d'ya reckon, mate?"
Said Harry Butler to Billy Cokebottle
The coon salooners have got nothing
On Einstein or Aristotle

So leave them be
To live the life they live
And if you think we're crazy
You've got a mind like a sieve

We're happy as pigs in shit
With nothing better to do
We've tried it and liked it, baby
I reckon we've got it easy, don't you?

The Character Jim

The character Jim, is instructed in cultural custom and ways of his people through the tutelage of his grandfather, Sam.

Jim's mother, Mary, is in the mourning room, wailing at the loss of her husband, Dave.

Mary is singing Dave's wals (sad) sing (song). This is a song that signifies remembering a person's soul)

The focus shifts out of the room and to the campfire, where Sam is sharing stories with Jim and Tilda.

Sam is telling the story of the first fire-as told in chapter 1-at the point of the lightning's strike. *He continues the story and explains the Wulgi's appointment of the Kadachi as spiritual guides in the physical realm.*

The wailing of Mary cuts the story short and the trio share in a moment of sadness. Sam, in an effort to console Jim on the loss of his father, Dave, tells a story which explains the path of a spirit after it has left the physical world. He explains that in putting the body to rest, the spirit will be able to recycle and rejoin the physical world in another form.

An eagle hawk perches itself on a sturdy tree branch and watches over the two. *Sam tells Jim of the rarity of seeing an eagle hawk and elaborates on their role as the messengers of the spirit world.*

Jim asks of the consequences if a soul were unable to find its way in the spirit realm and rebirth, to which Sam explains that there is no need to worry about that.

Sam leaves Tilda and Jim because he too, was young once and liked a girl.

Tilda tells Jim that she heard he was going to die when the **Rainbow** swallows him up, explaining that she has to hide when she hears its roar.

Jim's first aunt, Jenny, approaches and directs Jim to collect more firewood, and Tilda to round up the children for dinner.

After dinner a gathering forms at the communal fire for a performance. As the performance reaches its climax, Jims uncle, Ned, quickly abducts Jim for his initiation.

The Frog

'Well hello" I said to my new found friend
as I encountered him eye to eye'
"how's life and how's your missus been?"
a deep throated croak was his reply.
So I had to change my lingo
Into north westralian froganese
I offered my friend a couple of flies
And we talked as he savoured these.
He told me of life in the toilet block,
How competition was getting tough,
How he had to fight for his territory,
I thought he had things pretty rough.
A flick of his tongue, another bug caught
To be eaten at once with glee,
He said that food was abundant,
At least he got it for free.
He lived between the dark grey walls
Amid the systems, pipes and dirt,
He had a wife and umpteen kids
But occasionally he did flirt.
Then my time was up, I'd done the deed,
With a flush I moved to the door,
He said "I'll see ya later, old chum"
"and we'll sit and talk some more.

Why

I don't know why I write,
My words just don't make sense,
They seem to be all jumbled
In the past or future tense.

They're mostly of life and scenery
Or places I have been
I try to describe them as best as I can
And recapture the views that I've seen.

It's pretty hard though, with my memory
I really don't know why I try
But I try to remember the images
as the countryside goes by.

All scenery differs; no two views are the same,
It's hard to recapture them frame by frame.
But I'll keep on trying till the day I die,
Or at least until my pen runs dry.

For poems are a good way to express one's self
It keeps the mind in a good state of health
And if you don't like just one line of verse
Just tell me, and I'll write you one and make it perverse.

Time for Bed

For so long we've craved to sleep in a bed
Instead of the hard, lumpy ground
But what with the prices up here in Broome
Not even a haystack could be found

So back to the tent and the dirt
The five by seven plastic cell
Where the mattress is Mother Nature
And the mossies and ants give you hell

Where every time you want a coffee
Or something cooked to eat
You bust your arse over an open fire
Amid flies, dust, smoke and heat

But this morning all that changed
As we were on our way from the tent
We were offered a caravan for a week
With a special cut in the rent

The rent was usually two hundred and ten
But we could have it for one-fifty
What with the prospect of a bed and a fridge
And an electric stove, quite nifty

We didn't pay any cash for it
He had a proposition to make
The arrangement was a bargain
So his offer we did take

Our first night in the caravan
Looking forward to a good night's sleep
Without the lumps, ants and mossies
That, mate, you can keep
Broome WA Oct 84

Sunburn

After a day at the beach I feel rather sore
The sun came and burnt me where it's never before
My back and my legs are a deep dark red
I feel it now as I lay in my bed
The tossing and turning~the burning and pain
I never do want to see sunshine again.
But everyone does it~I'm sure you'll agree
There's nothing quite like a day at the sea.
So go to the beach and get cooked like a prawn
And later tonight you also will scorn.
The wind was too strong; the sun was too hot
You won't notice a thing til it's time for the cot.
But be careful; don't spend too long in the sun
Or you too will come home with a sunburnt bum.

Yes Sir and Three Bags Full

If we go to the city during the day
There are always people standing in the way,
They look us up and down as if we were scum
The daytime city, you can stick it chum.
Plastic people everywhere, looking down their nose
Where are they heading?, they don't know I don't suppose.
That they are all like clones, yes sir and three bags full
Running round like robots, trying to act cool.
But they are only jealous they can't do as they wish
Having it all served to them on a silver plated dish.
They don't know what it is to fight for existence and a feed,
They're all trying to outdo one another, like cannibalistic greed.
So let them be like daleks, yes sir and three bags full,
Us street people are lucky, we ain't no~one's fool.
Yet night time in the city is really something else
No~one there to hassle us, they're all home on the shelf.
Only a few street kids, wondering where to sleep
Night time city is the go, the daytime you can keep.
So next time you are in a bar, squatting on you're stool
Be grateful you're a street person, you ain't no~one's fool.
Just think of all the lookalikes, trying to act cool
And thank the lord that you ain't saying yes sir and three bags full.

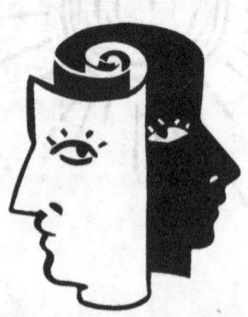

Zen

The sun shining thru', like a fragmented crystal
The mountain at peace
The leaves dancing round as the breeze gently flutters,
The day is fading far in the east.
The birds are all singing their afternoon song,
Making the music for one to enjoy,
The fresh mountain creeks, turquoise, clear and cold
With lush vegetation painted about.
Waterfalls, rocky, descending, perspiring,
The bushlife, the sanctuary and scenery intriguing.
A lizard on the roof, basking in the heat,
Bush turkeys looking for something to eat.
A mouthful of coffee, a toke on a pipe,
I'll sit here and watch the day become night.

Pay Day 2

Okay, that's sweet, what time will it be"
Twelve o'clock she says to come back
So you head for the door with a grin on your chin
And your mind's saying 'she'll be right, Jack"

I won't have to come back here for fourteen more days
To go through this bullshit again
It's a hard life working for the Government
Once a fortnight, with the stroke of a pen

Broome WA Dec 84

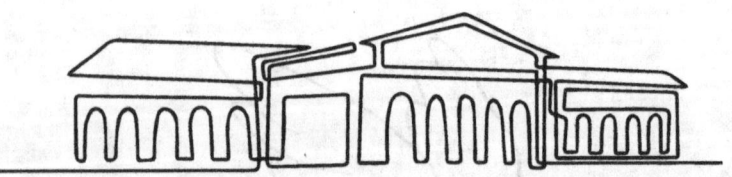

The Little Lebanese Leprechaun

We know a little leprechaun
And a Lebanese one at that
He wears a pair of black sunglasses
And a little green velvet hat.

He hangs around the waterfront
Or in the mall he waits
For all the little ladies
With whom he has made dates.

He really is a comic
A joke for different times
He's even getting to the stage
Where he laughs at all his crimes.

He's only been here three years
But he's travelled all this land
And when he returns home, one day
They'll get the news first hand.

With one bung nose and two black eyes
He toddles through the town
What with his back and the dose he got
That really brought him down.

But he'll get up and fight again
He always has before
And when his belly's full of wine
He'll sit and tell you the score.

With his little green hat and his sunglasses
People think he's quite potty
So leave him alone to drink in peace
Our little brother, Scotty.
Perth WA Mar 86

Wha's Like Us By Anon
Damn Few and They're a' Dead

An Englishman enjoys his breakfast of toast and **MARMALADE**- invented by Mrs Keilor of Dundee, Scotland.- reaches for his **RAINCOAT**- patented by Charles Macintosh from Glasgow, Scotland-to dash to the station on his **BICYCLE**-invented by Kirkpatrick Macmillan, blacksmith of Dumfries, Scotland-whose **TYRES**- invented by John Boyd Dunlop of Dreghorn, Scotland

The journey by train whose **STEAM ENGINE**- was invented by James Watt of Greenock, Scotland,- takes him to his work at **THE BANK OF ENGLAND**- founded by William Paterson of Dumfries, Scotland.

While opening his mail with **ADHESIVE STAMPS**- invented by James Chalmers fof Dundee, Scotland- he puffs on a **CIGARETTE**- first manufactured by by Robert Cloag of Perth, Scotland

He later rings his wife on a **TELEPHONE**-invented by Graham Alexander Bell, born in Edinburgh, Scotland, she tells him dinner will be his favourite; roast beef, from **ABERDEEN ANGUS** raised in Aberdeenshire, Scotland.

He arrives home to find his daughter watching **TELEVISION**- invented by John Logie Baird, of Helensburgh, Scotland- a programme on the **US NAVY**- founded by John Paul Jones of Kirkbean, Scotland-and his son reading **TREASURE ISLAND**- by Robert Louis Stevenson, of Edinburgh, Scotland- and, on lifting the BIBLE he finds the first name mentioned is a Scot-King James Vi, who authorised it's translation.

The Englishman is unable to turn from the ingenuity of the Scots. He could turn to **WHISKY**, but Scotland supplies the best, or to end it all he might put his head in a gas oven-**COAL GAS** was discovered by William Murdoch, of Ayr, Scotland.

He could shoot himself, but his **BREACH LOADING RIFLE** was invented by Captain Pat Ferguson, of Pitfours, Scotland.If unsuccessful, he could be injected with **PENICILLIN**- discovered by Alexander Fleming of Darvel, Scotland-or given an **ANAESTHETIC**- discovered by Sir James Young Simpson of Bathgate, Scotland.

His last hope; a transfusion of Scots blood, then he could ask

HERE'S TAE US, WHA'S LIKE US, DAMN FEW, AN' THEY'RE A' DEAD

The Ravenshoe Line

Hey lordy, lordy on the Ravenshoe line,
I'd like to stop and talk, but I ain't got the time
I got places to go and things to see
And if you're asking me why,
Well, I'll tell you "that's me"

I'm a travelling man and I like to move around,
There's no chance of me getting nailed to the ground.
I like to move around from coast to coast
And I've travelled this land, well almost.

There's a lot to be seen and people to meet,
I hope it's in the country and not a main street
Cos' the cities full of suckers
And folks who don't know better,
I know better as I've told you in this letter.

Hey, lordy, lordy on the Ravenshoe line
I'd like to stop and talk, but I ain't got the time.

Isn't Life a Bitch

Isn't life a bitch?
Just when you get it right,
Half your hair turns grey
And the rest falls out,
And that's just overnight.
When everything looks rosy
You've just got on top of the bills,
Fuck, no, that's not quite good enough
And out of the bag it spills.
The telephones due, the powers cut off
And the Rego's only two weeks away,
Then the Social Security cuts you off
Doesn't that just make your day?
Your chins on the ground, a real happy chap,
Your arseholes just starting to pucker,
You feel like the world owe's you a favour
By jeez, can't life be a fucker.
But there's always that distant, distant light
At the tapering end of the tunnel,
And there's no other way to get to it
Except through the narrow end of a funnel.
 Yet, if you told me your woes and I told ya mine
We'd be here for the rest of the week
But please, don't piss I my pocket too long
Cos, Buddy, I'm getting wet feet.

Why Wait

Why do so many people
waste away their lives
waiting for old age to come
for which only fifty per cent survives

The nine to five rut
at the office every day
working their little arses off
trying to earn their pay

Fifty years they usually try
And exist til retirement day
So they can travel and see this land
To them, this is all I can say.

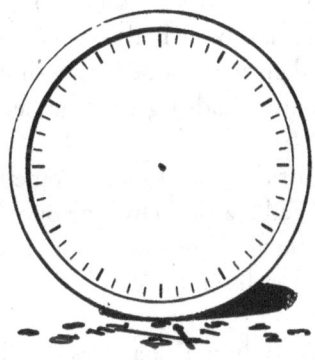

Why not do it now
Why wait for fifty long years
Why be stable and unhappy
Why put up a front for your fears.

Be happy, be free
Do your own sweet thing
Get out of the nine to five bullshit
Get out and give life a fling

Don't wait all of your life
To do what should be done now
But if you want to wait the fifty long years
You might make it there, somehow

Mt Hawthorn Aug 84

The Last Six Weeks *

Six weeks ago my life was a wreck
I had nothing to achieve or attain
An alcoholic at twenty-five
Never thought I'd be sober again

No place to call home, one blanket for warmth
On the side of the cold river bank
I can't blame no-one, the choice was made
I only had myself to thank

Striving to get drunk to beat the chilling wind
To numb the body from the weather
I'd given up hope for anything
I just couldn't get it together

Just three weeks later, something clicked
I had reason to live life once more
I hung up my flagon once and for all
I'd realised the score

Everything I'd had was lost through drink
Everyone I'd come to enhance
Then this lady I met had given me hope
I knew this was my one last chance

I don't want to lose her to fermented grapes
She don't want to lose me to the pills
Between us, I think, that we have made
Two determined, air tight wills

Take the city, the cops, the pills and the plonk
We don't want to know any of them
We're happy here by ourselves
We'll never be lonely again

I never knew life could be like this
Never valued my freedom so much
We've decided to give everything a miss
We'll keep each other, our love means too much

<u>Mosman Park April 84</u>